SONGS FOR EASY GUITAR

75 Hymns and Choruses

Compiled and Arranged
by DAVID WINKLER

Lillenas PUBLISHING COMPANY

KANSAS CITY, MO 64141

Rejoice in the Lord Always

1

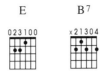

Words and Music by
EVELYN TARNER

Re - joice in the Lord_____ al - ways, and a - gain I say re -

joice! Re - joice in the Lord_____ al - ways, and a -

gain I say re - joice! Re - joice, re - joice, and a -

gain I say re - joice! Re - joice, re -

joice, and a - gain I say re - joice!

2 Bind Us Together

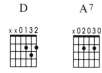

Words and Music by
BOB GILLMAN

Bind us to-geth-er, Lord; Bind us to-geth-er with
cords that can-not be bro - ken. Bind us to-
geth - er, Lord; Bind us to-geth-er, Lord; Bind us to-geth-er with
love. There is on - ly one God,
There is on - ly one King, There is on - ly one
Bod - y, That is why we can sing. Oh,

Oh, How I Love Jesus

3

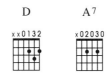

FREDERICK WHITFIELD

Traditional American Melody

Oh, how I love Je - sus. Oh, how I love Je - sus.

Oh, how I love Je - sus, Be - cause He first loved me.

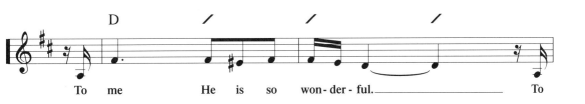

To me He is so won-der-ful. To

me He is so won-der-ful. To me He is so

won- der- ful, Be - cause He first loved me.

4 Hallowed Be Thy Name

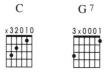

Words and Music by
BABBIE MASON and ROBERT LAWSON

You are love,___ You are life,___ You are Lord___ o - ver ev - 'ry - thing,

Al - pha, O - me - ga, Je - ho - vah, the King of Kings, Won - der - ful Way - mak - er, wor -

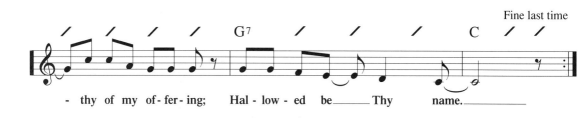

- thy of my of - fer - ing; Hal - low - ed be___ Thy name.___

1. You're the an - swer to all___ of my prob - lems and You solve them.
2. You're the al - might - y for - tress in a time of trib - u - la - tion.

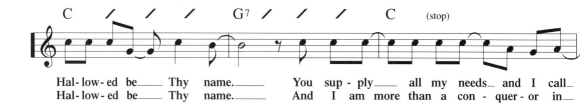

Hal - low - ed be___ Thy name.___ You sup - ply___ all my needs___ and I call___
Hal - low - ed be___ Thy name.___ And I am more than a con - quer - or in___

_You "Ab- ba, Fa - ther." Hal- low- ed be___ Thy name.___
ev- 'ry sit - u - a - tion. Hal- low- ed be___ Thy name.

King of Kings

5

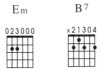

SOPHIE CONTY and NAOMI BATYA

Ancient Hebrew Folksong

King of Kings and Lord of___ Lords– Glo - ry, hal - le - lu - jah!

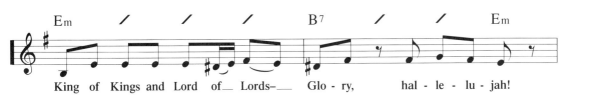

King of Kings and Lord of___ Lords– Glo - ry, hal - le - lu - jah!

Je - sus, Prince of Peace–___ Glo - ry, hal - le - lu - jah!

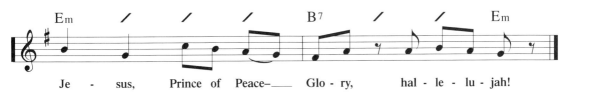

Je - sus, Prince of Peace–___ Glo - ry, hal - le - lu - jah!

6 Servant of All

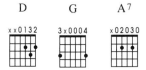

Words and Music by
MICHAEL RYAN

If you want to be great in God's king-dom, Learn to be the ser-vant of

all. If you want to be great in God's king - dom,

Learn to be the ser - vant of all. Learn to be the ser - vant of

all._____ Learn to be the ser - vant of all. If you want to be

great in God's king - dom, Learn to be the ser - vant of all._____

This Little Light of Mine

7

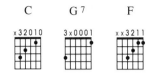

Traditional

Traditional

This lit-tle light of mine– I'm gon-na let it shine.

This lit-tle light of mine– I'm gon-na let it shine, let it

shine, let it shine, let it shine.

1. Hide it un-der a bush-el? No! I'm gon-na let it shine.
2. Don't let Sa-tan blow it out– I'm gon-na let it shine.
3. Let it shine till Je-sus comes– I'm gon-na let it shine.

Hide it un-der a bush-el? No! I'm gon-na let it shine, let it
Don't let Sa-tan blow it out– I'm gon-na let it shine, let it
Let it shine till Je-sus comes– I'm gon-na let it shine, let it

shine, let it shine, let it shine.
shine, let it shine, let it shine.
shine, let it shine, let it shine.

8 Behold What Manner of Love

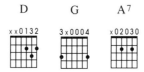

Words and Music by
PATRICIA VAN TINE

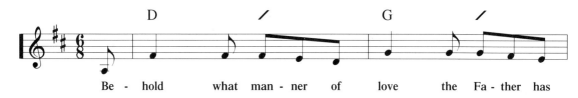

Be - hold what man - ner of love the Fa - ther has

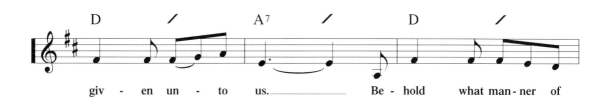

giv - en un - to us. Be - hold what man - ner of

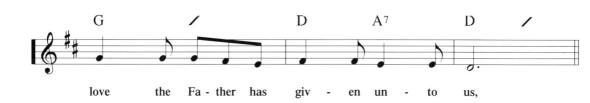

love the Fa - ther has giv - en un - to us,

That we should be called the sons of God,

That we should be called the sons of God.

Redeemed

9

G   D 7   C

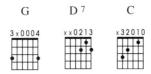

FANNY J. CROSBY

WILLIAM J. KIRKPATRICK

1. Re-deemed, how I love to pro-claim it! Re-deemed by the blood of the Lamb;_____ Re-deemed thro' His in-fi-nite mer-cy, His child, and for-ev-er, I am._____
2. Re-deemed and so hap-py in Je-sus, No lan-guage my rap-ture can tell;_____ I know that the light of His pres-ence With me doth con-tin-ual-ly dwell._____
3. I think of my bless-ed Re-deem-er, I think of Him all the day long;_____ I sing, for I can-not be si-lent; His love is the theme of my song._____
4. I know I shall see in His beau-ty The King in whose law I de-light;_____ Who lov-ing-ly guard-eth my foot-steps, And giv-eth me songs in the night._____

Refrain

Re-deemed,_____ re-deemed,_____ re-deemed by the blood of the Lamb;_____ Re-deemed, re-deemed,_____ His child, and for-ev-er, I am._____

10 Savior, like a Shepherd Lead Us

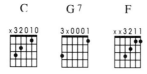

DOROTHY A. THRUPP   WILLIAM B. BRADBURY

1. Sav - ior, like a shep-herd lead___ us,___ Much we need Thy ten-der
2. We are Thine; do Thou be - friend___ us.___ Be the Guard-ian of our
3. Thou hast prom-ised to re - ceive___ us,___ Poor and sin - ful tho' we
4. Ear - ly let us seek Thy fa - vor;___ Ear - ly let us do Thy

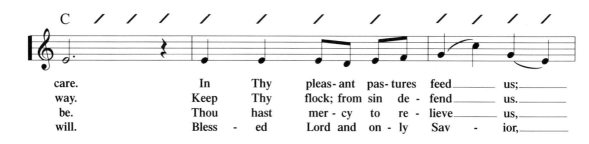

care.   In   Thy   pleas-ant pas-tures feed_____ us;_____
way.   Keep   Thy   flock; from sin de - fend_____ us._____
be.   Thou   hast   mer - cy to re - lieve_____ us,_____
will.   Bless - ed   Lord and on - ly Sav - ior,_____

For   our   use Thy folds pre - pare.   Bless-ed Je - sus,   bless-ed
Seek   us   when we go a - stray.   Bless-ed Je - sus,   bless-ed
Grace to   cleanse, and pow'r to free. Bless-ed Je - sus,   bless-ed
With   Thy   love our bos-oms fill.   Bless-ed Je - sus,   bless-ed

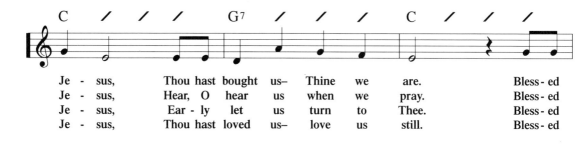

Je - sus,   Thou hast bought us– Thine we are.   Bless-ed
Je - sus,   Hear, O hear us when we pray.   Bless-ed
Je - sus,   Ear - ly let us turn to Thee.   Bless-ed
Je - sus,   Thou hast loved us– love us still.   Bless-ed

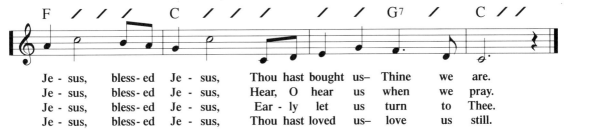

Je - sus, bless-ed Je - sus, Thou hast bought us— Thine we are.
Je - sus, bless-ed Je - sus, Hear, O hear us when we pray.
Je - sus, bless-ed Je - sus, Ear - ly let us turn to Thee.
Je - sus, bless-ed Je - sus, Thou hast loved us— love us still.

Through It All

11

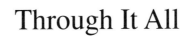

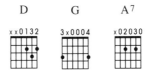

Words and Music by
ANDRAÉ CROUCH

Through it all,_____ through it all,_____ I've

learned to trust in Je - sus, I've learned to trust in God._____

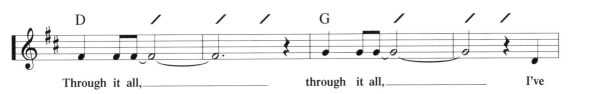

Through it all,_____ through it all,_____ I've

learned to de - pend_____ up - on His Word._____

12

The Unclouded Day

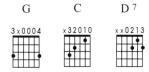

Words and Music by
Rev. J. K. ALWOOD

1. Oh, they tell me of a home far be-yond the skies; Oh, they
2. Oh, they tell me of a home where my friends have gone; Oh, they
3. Oh, they tell me of a King in His beau-ty there, And they
4. Oh, they tell me that He smiles on His chil-dren there, And His

tell me of a home__ far a-way; Oh, they tell me of a home where no
tell me of a land__ far a-way; Where the tree__ of__ life in e-
tell me that mine eyes__ shall be-hold Where He sits__ on the throne that is
smile__ drives their sor-rows all a-way; And they tell me that no tears ev-er

storm - clouds rise; Oh, they tell me of an un - cloud-ed day.
ter - nal bloom Sheds its fra - grance thro' the un - cloud-ed day.
whit - er than snow In the cit - y that is made of__ gold.
come__ a - gain In that love - ly land of un - cloud-ed day.

Refrain

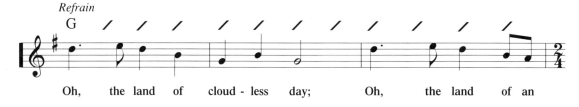

Oh, the land of cloud - less day; Oh, the land of an

un - cloud - ed sky. Oh, they tell me of a home where no

storm-clouds rise; Oh, they tell me of an un-cloud-ed day.

Nothing But the Blood

13

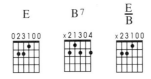

Words and Music by
ROBERT LOWRY

1. What can wash a - way my sin? Noth-ing but the blood of Je - sus.
2. For my par-don, this I see– Noth-ing but the blood of Je - sus.
3. Noth-ing can for sin a-tone– Noth-ing but the blood of Je - sus.
4. This is all my hope and peace– Noth-ing but the blood of Je - sus.

What can make me whole a - gain? Noth-ing but the blood of Je - sus.
For my cleans-ing, this my plea– Noth-ing but the blood of Je - sus.
Naught of good that I have done– Noth-ing but the blood of Je - sus.
This is all my righ-teous-ness– Noth-ing but the blood of Je - sus.

Refrain

Oh, pre - cious is the flow That makes me white as snow.

No oth-er fount I know– Noth-ing but the blood of Je - sus.

Alleluia

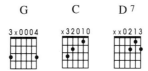

Words and Music by
JERRY SINCLAIR

1. Al - le - lu - ia, Al - le - lu - ia, Al - le -
2. He's my Sav - ior, He's my Sav - ior, He's my
3. I will praise Him, I will praise Him, I will

lu - ia, Al - le - lu - ia, Al - le - lu - ia, Al - le -
Sav - ior, He's my Sav - ior, He's my Sav - ior, He's my
praise Him, I will praise Him, I will praise Him, I will

lu - ia, Al - le - lu - ia, Al - le - lu - ia!
Sav - ior, He's my Sav - ior, He's my Sav - ior!
praise Him, I will praise Him, I will praise Him!

Father, I Adore You

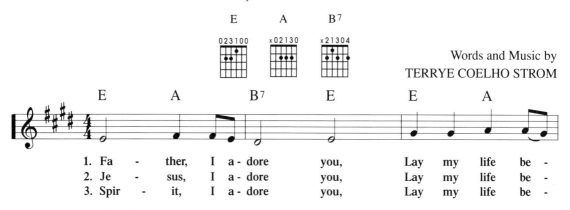

Words and Music by
TERRYE COELHO STROM

1. Fa - ther, I a - dore you, Lay my life be -
2. Je - sus, I a - dore you, Lay my life be -
3. Spir - it, I a - dore you, Lay my life be -

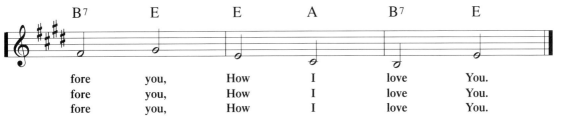

fore you, How I love You.
fore you, How I love You.
fore you, How I love You.

It Is a Good Thing to Give Thanks 16

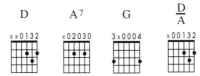

Words and Music by
JUDY HORNER MONTEMAYOR

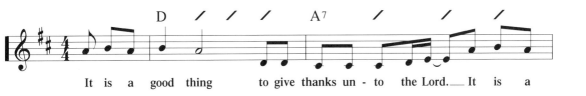

It is a good thing to give thanks un - to the Lord. It is a

good thing to give thanks un - to the Lord, And to sing

prais - es un - to Thy name, O Most High.

17 Higher Ground

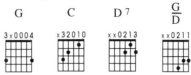

JOHNSON OATMAN, Jr.   CHARLES H. GABRIEL

1. I'm press-ing on the up-ward way; New heights I'm
2. My heart has no de-sire to stay Where doubts a-
3. I want to live a-bove the world, Tho' Sa-tan's
4. I want to scale the ut-most height And catch a

gain - ing ev-'ry day– Still pray-ing as I'm on-ward
rise and fears dis-may; Tho' some may dwell where these a-
darts at me are hurled; For faith has caught the joy-ful
gleam of glo-ry bright; But still I'll pray till heav'n I've

bound, "Lord, plant my feet on high - er ground."
bound, My prayer, my aim, is high - er ground.
sound, The song of saints on high - er ground.
found, "Lord, lead me on to high - er ground."

Refrain

Lord, lift me up and let me stand By faith on heav - en's ta-ble-

land; A high-er plane than I have found– Lord, plant my feet on high-er ground.

Down in My Heart

18

A   E7   A7   D

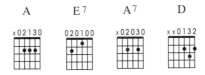

Words and Music by
GEORGE W. COOKE

1. I have the joy,___ joy,___ joy,___ joy___ down in my heart,
2. I have the peace that pass-es un-der-stand-ing down in my heart,
3. I have the love of Je-sus, love of Je-sus down in my heart,

Down in my heart, down in my heart. I have the joy,___ joy,___ joy,___ joy___
Down in my heart, down in my heart. I have the peace that pass-es un-der-stand-ing
Down in my heart, down in my heart. I have the love of Je-sus, love of Je-sus

down in my heart, Down in my heart to stay. And I'm so hap-py, so ver-y
down in my heart, Down in my heart to stay.
down in my heart, Down in my heart to stay.

hap-py; I have the love of Je-sus in my heart, down in my heart. And I'm so

hap-py, so ver-y hap-py; I have the love of Je-sus in my heart.___

19

Only Trust Him

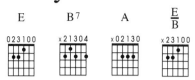

Words and Music by
JOHN H. STOCKTON

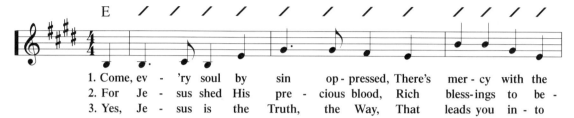

1. Come, ev - 'ry soul by sin op - pressed, There's mer - cy with the
2. For Je - sus shed His pre - cious blood, Rich bless - ings to be -
3. Yes, Je - sus is the Truth, the Way, That leads you in - to

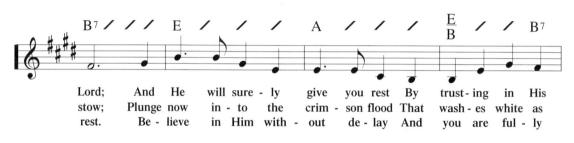

Lord; And He will sure - ly give you rest By trust - ing in His
stow; Plunge now in - to the crim - son flood That wash - es white as
rest. Be - lieve in Him with - out de - lay And you are ful - ly

Refrain

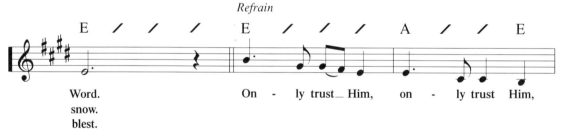

Word. On - ly trust Him, on - ly trust Him,
snow.
blest.

On - ly trust Him now. He will save you,

He will save you, He will save you now.

I've Been Redeemed

20

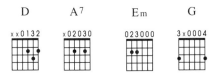

Unknown

Unknown

I've been re-deemed   by the blood of the

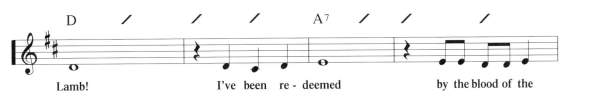

Lamb!   I've been re-deemed   by the blood of the

Lamb!   I've been re-deemed by the blood of the

Lamb— Filled with the Ho-ly Ghost I am.   All my

sins are washed a-way— I've been re-deemed.

21

Unto Thee, O Lord

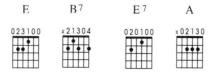

Based on Psalm 25:1-6

CHARLES F. MONROE

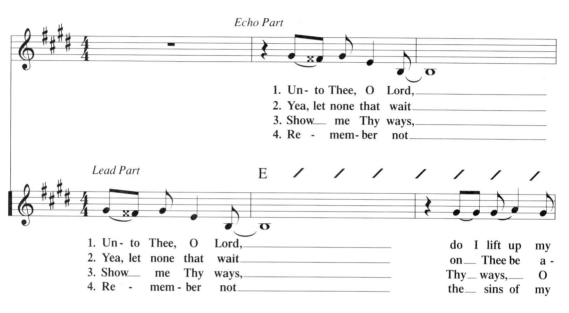

Echo Part

1. Un - to Thee, O Lord,
2. Yea, let none that wait
3. Show_ me Thy ways,
4. Re - mem - ber not

Lead Part

E

1. Un - to Thee, O Lord, ___ do I lift up my
2. Yea, let none that wait ___ on_ Thee be a -
3. Show_ me Thy ways, ___ Thy_ ways,_ O
4. Re - mem - ber not ___ the_ sins of my

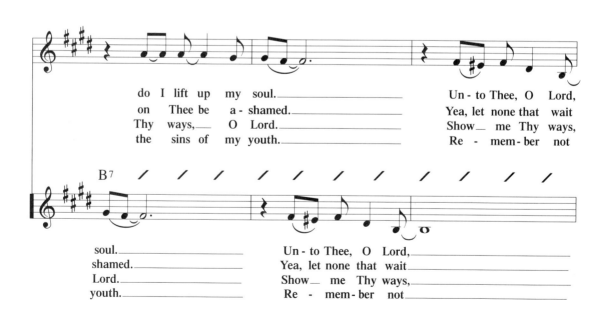

do I lift up my soul.___ Un - to Thee, O Lord,
on Thee be a - shamed.___ Yea, let none that wait
Thy ways,_ O Lord.___ Show_ me Thy ways,
the sins of my youth.___ Re - mem - ber not

B7

soul.___ Un - to Thee, O Lord, ___
shamed.___ Yea, let none that wait ___
Lord.___ Show_ me Thy ways, ___
youth.___ Re - mem - ber not ___

22 The Battle Belongs to the Lord

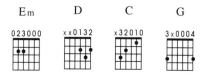

Words and Music by
JAMIE OWENS-COLLINS

1. In heav-en-ly ar - mor we'll en - ter the land— The
2. When the pow-er of dark - ness comes in like a flood, The
3. When your en-e-my press-es in hard, do not fear— The

bat - tle be-longs to the Lord. No wea-pon that's fash - ioned a-gainst
bat - tle be-longs to the Lord. He's raised up a stan - dard, the pow'r
bat - tle be-longs to the Lord. Take cour-age, my friend, your re-demp-

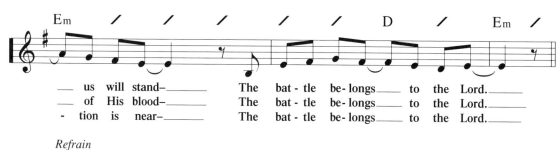

us will stand— The bat - tle be-longs to the Lord.
of His blood— The bat - tle be-longs to the Lord.
tion is near— The bat - tle be-longs to the Lord.

Refrain

And we sing glo - ry, hon - or, pow- er and strength to the Lord.

We sing glo - ry, hon - or, pow- er and strength to the Lord.

Revive Us Again

23

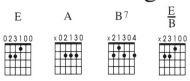

WILLIAM P. MACKAY

JOHN J. HUSBAND

1. We praise Thee, O God, for the Son of Thy love, For Jesus who died and is now gone above.
2. We praise Thee, O God, for Thy Spirit of light, Who has shown us our Savior and scattered our night.
3. All glory and praise to the Lamb that was slain, Who has borne all our sins and has cleansed ev'ry stain.
4. Revive us again– fill each heart with Thy love. May each soul be rekindled with fire from above.

Refrain

Hallelujah! Thine the glory! Hallelujah! Amen! Hallelujah! Thine the glory! Revive us again.

24

Take My Life

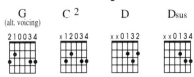

Words and Music by
SCOTT UNDERWOOD

1. Ho - li - ness, ho - li - ness is what I long for;
2. Faith- ful - ness, faith-ful - ness is what I long for;
3. Righ- teous- ness, righ-teous-ness is what I long for;

Ho - li - ness is what I need.
Faith - ful - ness is what I need.
Righ- teous- ness is what I need.

Ho - li - ness, ho - li - ness is what You want from me.
Faith - ful - ness, faith-ful - ness is what You want from me.
Righ- teous- ness, righ-teous - ness is what You want from me.

Take my

heart and form it; Take my mind— trans -

form it; Take my will— con - form it

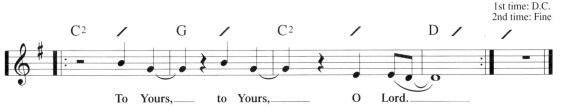

To Yours,____ to Yours,____ O Lord.____

I Will Bless Thee, O Lord

25

Words and Music by
ESTHER WATANABE

I will bless Thee, O Lord.____ I will bless Thee, O

Lord.____ With a heart of thanks - giv - 'ing____

___ I will bless Thee, O Lord.____ With my hands lift- ed

up____ And my mouth filled with praise,____

___ With a heart of thanks- giv - ing____ I will bless Thee, O Lord.____

26 There Is Power in the Blood

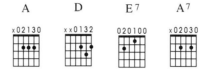

Words and Music by
LEWIS E. JONES

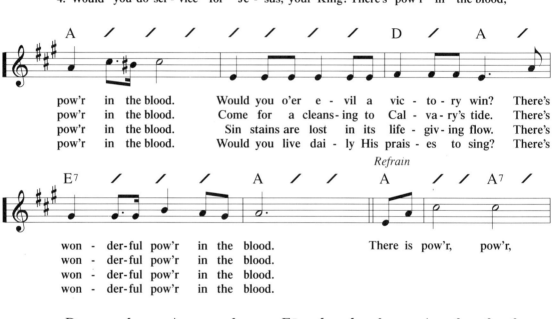

1. Would you be free from your bur-den of sin? There's pow'r in the blood,
2. Would you be free from your pas-sion and pride? There's pow'r in the blood,
3. Would you be whit-er, much whit-er than snow? There's pow'r in the blood,
4. Would you do ser-vice for Je-sus, your King? There's pow'r in the blood,

pow'r in the blood. Would you o'er e-vil a vic-to-ry win? There's
pow'r in the blood. Come for a cleans-ing to Cal-va-ry's tide. There's
pow'r in the blood. Sin stains are lost in its life-giv-ing flow. There's
pow'r in the blood. Would you live dai-ly His prais-es to sing? There's

Refrain

won-der-ful pow'r in the blood. There is pow'r, pow'r,
won-der-ful pow'r in the blood.
won-der-ful pow'r in the blood.
won-der-ful pow'r in the blood.

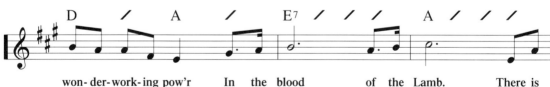

won-der-work-ing pow'r In the blood of the Lamb. There is

pow'r, pow'r, won-der-work-ing pow'r In the pre-cious blood of the Lamb.

This Is My Commandment

27

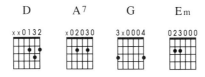

Adapted from John 15:11, 12

Unknown

This is my com-mand-ment: That you love one an-

oth-er, That your joy may be full.

full. That your joy may be

full, That your joy may be

full. This is my com-mand-ment: That you love one an-

oth-er, That your joy may be full.

28 The Joy of the Lord

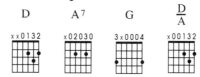

Words and Music by
ALLIENE G. VALE

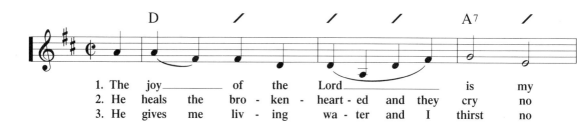

1. The joy_____ of the Lord_____ is my
2. He heals the bro - ken - heart - ed and they cry no
3. He gives me liv - ing wa - ter and I thirst no

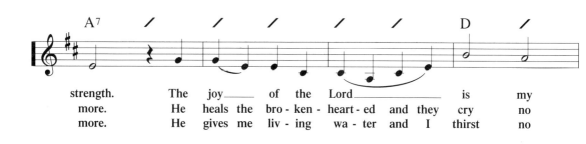

strength. The joy_____ of the Lord_____ is my
more. He heals the bro - ken - heart - ed and they cry no
more. He gives me liv - ing wa - ter and I thirst no

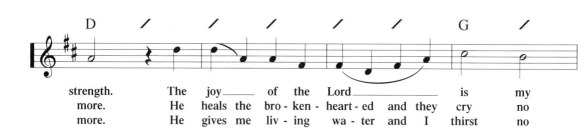

strength. The joy_____ of the Lord_____ is my
more. He heals the bro - ken - heart - ed and they cry no
more. He gives me liv - ing wa - ter and I thirst no

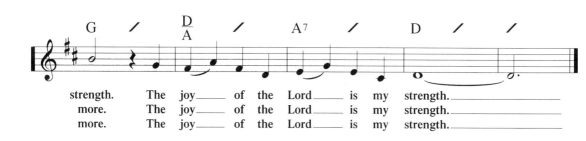

strength. The joy_____ of the Lord_____ is my strength._____
more. The joy_____ of the Lord_____ is my strength._____
more. The joy_____ of the Lord_____ is my strength._____

Shall We Gather at the River?

Words and Music by
ROBERT LOWRY

1. Shall we gath-er at the riv - er, Where bright an-gel feet have
2. On the mar-gin of the riv - er, Wash - ing up its sil - ver
3. Ere we reach the shin-ing riv - er, Lay we ev - 'ry bur-den
4. Soon we'll reach the shin-ing riv - er; Soon our pil-grim-age will

trod;_____ With its crys-tal tide for-ev - er Flow-ing
spray,_____ We will walk and wor-ship ev - er, All the
down;_____ Grace our spir-its will de-liv - er, And pro-
cease._____ Soon our hap-py hearts will quiv - er With the

by the_ throne of_ God?
hap-py_ gold-en_ day.
vide a_ robe and_ crown.
mel-o-dy of_ peace.

Refrain

Yes, we'll gath-er at the

riv - er, The beau-ti-ful, the beau-ti-ful_____ riv - er;

Gath-er with the saints_ at the riv - er That flows by the throne of_ God.

30

They'll Know We Are Christians by Our Love

Words and Music by
PETER SCHOLTES

1. We are one in the Spir - it; we are one in the Lord. We are one in the Spir - it; we are one in the Lord. And we pray that all u - ni - ty may one day be re - stored.

2. We will walk with each oth - er; we will walk hand in hand. We will walk with each oth - er; we will walk hand in hand, And to - geth - er we'll spread the news that God is in our land.

3. We will work with each oth - er; we will work side by side. We will work with each oth - er; we will work side by side, And we'll guard each man's dig - ni - ty and save each man's pride.

4. All praise to the Fa - ther from whom all things come; And all praise to Christ Je - sus, His on - ly Son; And all praise to the Spir - it who makes us one.

Refrain

And they'll know we are Chris - tians by our love, by our love; Yes, they'll know we are Chris - tians by our love.

At the Cross

31

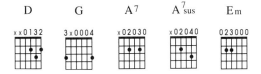

ISAAC WATTS; refrain, RALPH E. HUDSON

RALPH E. HUDSON

1. A - las! and did my Sav - ior bleed? And did my Sov'reign die? Would
2. Was it for crimes that I have done He groaned up - on the tree? A -
3. Well might the sun in dark - ness hide And shut His glo - ries in, When
4. But drops of grief can ne'er re - pay The debt of love I owe. Here,

He de - vote that sa - cred head For sin - ners such as I?
maz - ing pit - y! grace un - known! And love be - yond de - gree!
Christ, the might - y Mak - er, died For man the crea - ture's sin.
Lord, I give my - self a - way– 'Tis all that I can do.

Refrain

At the cross, at the cross where I first saw the light, And the

bur - den of my heart rolled a - way, It was there by faith I re -

ceived my sight, And now I am hap - py all the day.

32 Have Thine Own Way, Lord

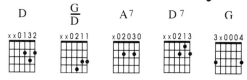

ADELAINE A. POLLARD

GEORGE C. STEBBINS

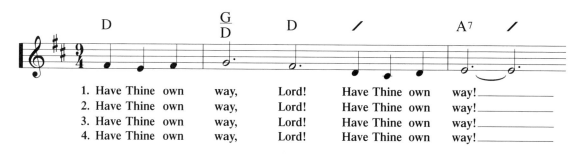

1. Have Thine own way, Lord! Have Thine own way!
2. Have Thine own way, Lord! Have Thine own way!
3. Have Thine own way, Lord! Have Thine own way!
4. Have Thine own way, Lord! Have Thine own way!

Thou art the Pot - ter, I am the clay.
Search me and try me, Mas - ter, to - day!
Wound - ed and wea - ry, help me, I pray!
Hold o'er my be - ing ab - so - lute sway!

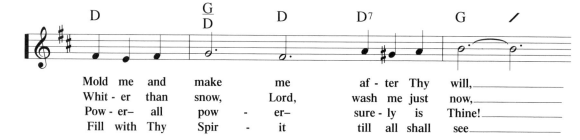

Mold me and make me af - ter Thy will,
Whit - er than snow, Lord, wash me just now,
Pow - er— all pow - er— sure - ly is Thine!
Fill with Thy Spir - it till all shall see

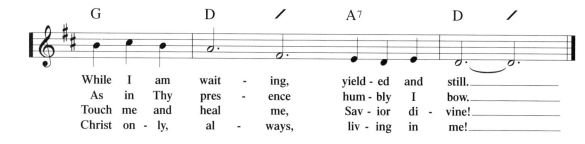

While I am wait - ing, yield - ed and still.
As in Thy pres - ence hum - bly I bow.
Touch me and heal me, Sav - ior di - vine!
Christ on - ly, al - ways, liv - ing in me!

Emmanuel

33

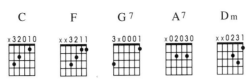

Words and Music by
BOB McGEE

Em - man - u - el,   Em - man - u -

el,   His name is called

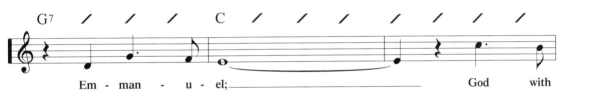

Em - man - u - el;   God with

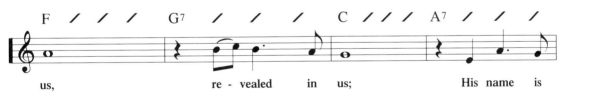

us,   re - vealed in us;   His name is

called   Em - man - u - el.

34 Are You Washed in the Blood?

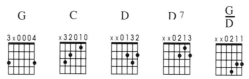

Words and Music by
ELISHA A. HOFFMAN

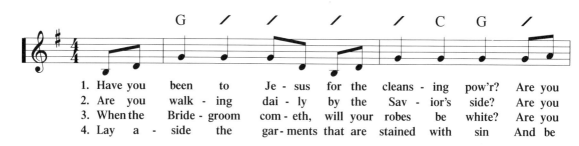

1. Have you been to Je - sus for the cleans - ing pow'r? Are you
2. Are you walk - ing dai - ly by the Sav - ior's side? Are you
3. When the Bride - groom com - eth, will your robes be white? Are you
4. Lay a - side the gar - ments that are stained with sin And be

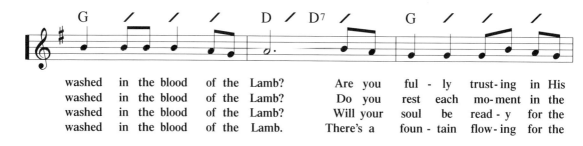

washed in the blood of the Lamb? Are you ful - ly trust-ing in His
washed in the blood of the Lamb? Do you rest each mo-ment in the
washed in the blood of the Lamb? Will your soul be read - y for the
washed in the blood of the Lamb. There's a foun - tain flow-ing for the

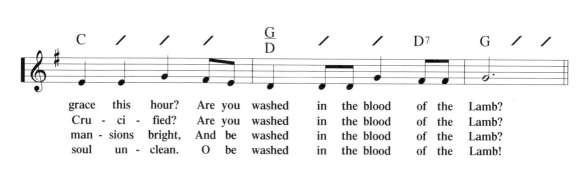

grace this hour? Are you washed in the blood of the Lamb?
Cru - ci - fied? Are you washed in the blood of the Lamb?
man - sions bright, And be washed in the blood of the Lamb?
soul un - clean. O be washed in the blood of the Lamb!

Refrain

Are you washed in the blood, In the

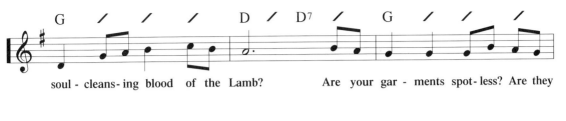

soul - cleans- ing blood of the Lamb? Are your gar - ments spot- less? Are they

white as snow? Are you washed in the blood of the Lamb?

God Is So Good

35

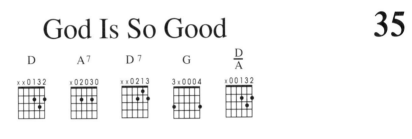

Traditional

Traditional

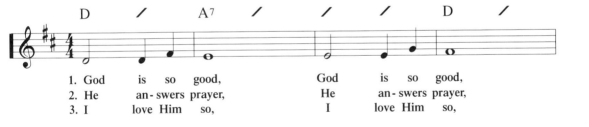

1. God   is   so   good,   God   is   so   good,
2. He   an- swers prayer,   He   an- swers prayer,
3. I   love Him   so,   I   love Him   so,

God   is   so   good,   He's so good   to   me.
He   an- swers prayer,   He's so good   to   me.
I   love Him   so,   He's so good   to   me.

36 Hallelu, Hallelujah!

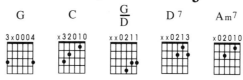

Traditional   Traditional

Hal- le - lu,   hal-le-lu,   hal-le-lu,   hal-le-lu - jah,   Praise   ye   the

Lord.   Hal- le - lu,   hal- le-lu,   hal-le - lu,   hal- le - lu - jah,

Praise   ye   the Lord.   Praise   ye   the

Lord,   hal- le - lu - jah,   Praise   ye   the Lord,   hal- le - lu - jah,

Praise   ye   the Lord,   hal- le - lu - jah,   Praise   ye   the Lord.

Kum Ba Yah

(Come By Here)

37

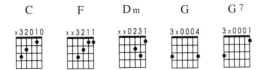

Traditional

African Melody

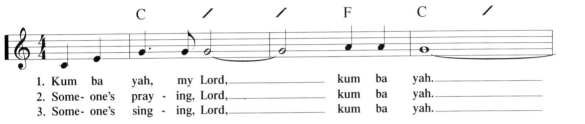

1. Kum ba yah, my Lord,_____ kum ba yah._____
2. Some-one's pray - ing, Lord,_____ kum ba yah._____
3. Some-one's sing - ing, Lord,_____ kum ba yah._____

____ Kum ba yah, my Lord,_____ kum ba yah._____
____ Some-one's pray - ing, Lord,_____ kum ba yah._____
____ Some-one's sing - ing, Lord,_____ kum ba yah._____

____ Kum ba yah, my Lord,_____ kum ba yah._____
____ Some-one's pray - ing, Lord,_____ kum ba yah._____
____ Some-one's sing - ing, Lord,_____ kum ba yah._____

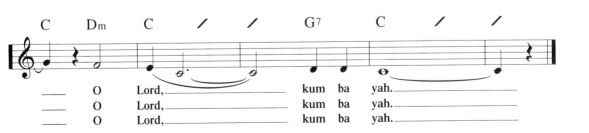

____ O Lord,_____ kum ba yah._____
____ O Lord,_____ kum ba yah._____
____ O Lord,_____ kum ba yah._____

38 Peace Like a River

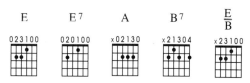

Traditional   Traditional

1. I've got peace like a riv-er, I've got peace like a
2. I've got love like an o-cean, I've got love like an
3. I've got joy like a foun-tain, I've got joy like a

riv-er, I've got peace like a riv-er in my
o-cean, I've got love like an o-cean in my
foun-tain, I've got joy like a foun-tain in my

soul. I've got peace like a
soul. I've got love like an
soul. I've got joy like a

riv-er, I've got peace like a riv-er, I've got
o-cean, I've got love like an o-cean, I've got
foun-tain, I've got joy like a foun-tain, I've got

peace like a riv-er in my soul.
love like an o-cean in my soul.
joy like a foun-tain in my soul.

Sweet By and By

39

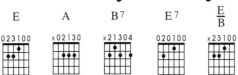

SANFORD F. BENNETT

JOSEPH P. WEBSTER

1. There's a land that is fair - er than day, And by
2. We shall sing on that beau - ti - ful shore The me -
3. To our boun - ti - ful Fa - ther a - bove We will

faith we can see it a - far; For the Fa - ther waits o - ver the
lo - di - ous songs of the blest; And our spir - its shall sor - row no
of - fer our trib - ute of praise, For the glo - ri - ous gift of His

way To pre - pare us a dwell - ing place there.
more– Not a sigh for the bless - ing of rest.
love And the bless - ings that hal - low our days.

Refrain

In the sweet by and by, We shall meet on that beau - ti - ful

shore. In the sweet by and by, We shall meet on that beau - ti - ful shore.

40

Jesus Loves Me

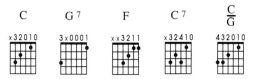

ANNA B. WARNER, alt.

WILLIAM B. BRADBURY

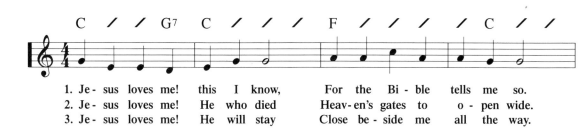

1. Je - sus loves me! this I know, For the Bi - ble tells me so.
2. Je - sus loves me! He who died Heav - en's gates to o - pen wide.
3. Je - sus loves me! He will stay Close be - side me all the way.

Lit - tle ones to Him be - long; They are weak, but He is strong.
He will wash a - way my sin, Let His lit - tle child come in.
If I love Him, when I die He will take me home on high.

Refrain

Yes, Je - sus loves me! Yes, Je - sus loves me!

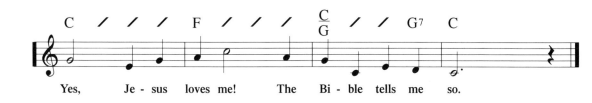

Yes, Je - sus loves me! The Bi - ble tells me so.

I Will Bless the Lord at All Times

41

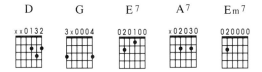

Words and Music by
JEANIE CLATTENBURG

I will bless the Lord⎯ at all⎯ times. I will bless the Lord⎯ at

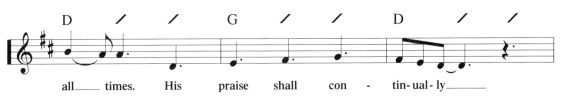

all⎯ times. His praise shall con - tin-ual-ly⎯

be in my mouth. I will bless the Lord⎯ at

all⎯ times. I will bless the Lord⎯ at all⎯ times. His

praise shall con - tin-ual-ly⎯ be in my mouth.

42

There Is a Fountain

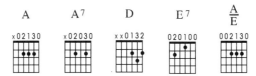

WILLIAM COWPER

Traditional American Melody

1. There is a foun-tain filled with blood Drawn from Im-man-uel's
2. The dy-ing thief re-joiced to see That foun-tain in his
3. E'er since by faith I saw the stream Thy flow-ing wounds sup-
4. When this poor lisp-ing, stam-m'ring tongue Lies si-lent in the

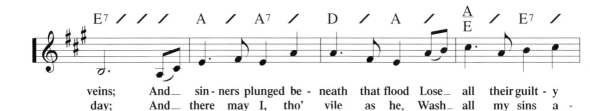

veins; And sin-ners plunged be-neath that flood Lose all their guilt-y
day; And there may I, tho' vile as he, Wash all my sins a-
ply, Re-deem-ing love has been my theme And shall be till I
grave, Then in a no-bler, sweet-er song I'll sing Thy pow'r to

stains. Lose all their guilt-y stains, Lose all their guilt-y stains; And
way. Wash all my sins a-way, Wash all my sins a-way; And
die. And shall be till I die, And shall be till I die; Re-
save. I'll sing Thy pow'r to save. I'll sing Thy pow'r to save. Then

sin-ners plunged be-neath that flood Lose all their guilt-y stains.
there may I, tho' vile as he, Wash all my sins a-way.
deem-ing love has been my theme And shall be till I die.
in a no-bler, sweet-er song I'll sing Thy pow'r to save.

What a Friend We Have in Jesus

43

JOSEPH M. SCRIVEN

CHARLES C. CONVERSE

1. What a Friend we have in Je - sus, All our sins and griefs to bear!
2. Have we tri - als and temp - ta - tions? Is there trou - ble an - y - where?
3. Are we weak and heav - y - la - den, Cum - bered with a load of care?

What a priv - i - lege to car - ry Ev - 'ry - thing to God in prayer!
We should nev - er be dis - cour - aged; Take it to the Lord in prayer.
Pre - cious Sav - ior, still our Ref - uge– Take it to the Lord in prayer.

Oh, what peace we of - ten for - feit, Oh, what need - less pain we bear,
Can we find a friend so faith - ful Who will all our sor - rows share?
Do thy friends de - spise, for - sake thee? Take it to the Lord in prayer.

All be - cause we do not car - ry Ev - 'ry - thing to God in prayer!
Je - sus knows our ev - 'ry weak - ness; Take it to the Lord in prayer.
In His arms He'll take and shield thee; Thou wilt find a sol - ace there.

44 Thy Loving Kindness

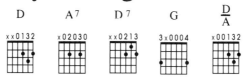

H.M., based on Ps. 63:3-4

HUGH MITCHELL

1. Thy lov - ing kind - ness____ is bet - ter than life.
2. I lift my hands, Lord,____ un - to Thy name.

Thy lov - ing kind - ness____ is bet - ter than
I lift my hands, Lord,____ un - to Thy

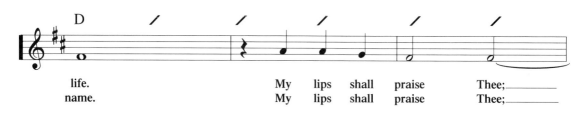

life. My lips shall praise Thee;____
name. My lips shall praise Thee;____

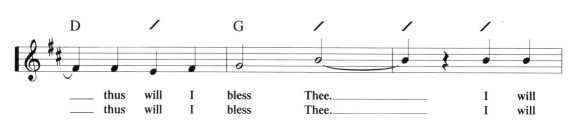

____ thus will I bless Thee.____ I will
____ thus will I bless Thee.____ I will

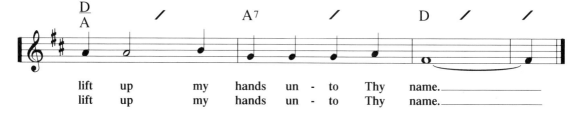

lift up my hands un - to Thy name.____
lift up my hands un - to Thy name.____

Leaning on the Everlasting Arms   45

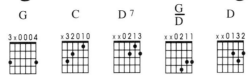

ELISHA A. HOFFMAN

ANTHONY J. SHOWALTER

1. What a fel-low-ship, what a joy di-vine, Lean-ing on the ev-er-last-ing arms; What a bless-ed-ness, what a peace is mine,
2. Oh, how sweet to walk in this pil-grim way, Lean-ing on the ev-er-last-ing arms; Oh, how bright the path grows from day to day,
3. What have I to dread, what have I to fear, Lean-ing on the ev-er-last-ing arms? I have bless-ed peace with my Lord so near,

Refrain

Lean-ing on the ev-er-last-ing arms. Lean - ing,
Lean-ing on the ev-er-last-ing arms.
Lean-ing on the ev-er-last-ing arms.

lean - ing, Safe and se-cure from all a-larms;

Lean - ing, lean - ing, Lean-ing on the ev-er-last-ing arms.

46 I Have Decided to Follow Jesus

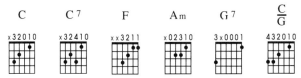

Anonymous

Folk Melody from India

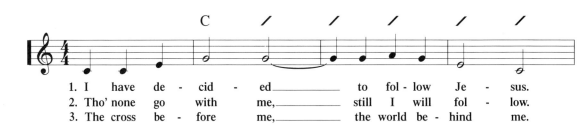

1. I have de - cid - ed to fol - low Je - sus.
2. Tho' none go with me, still I will fol - low.
3. The cross be - fore me, the world be - hind me.

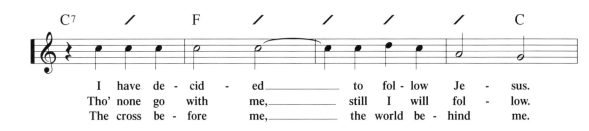

I have de - cid - ed to fol - low Je - sus.
Tho' none go with me, still I will fol - low.
The cross be - fore me, the world be - hind me.

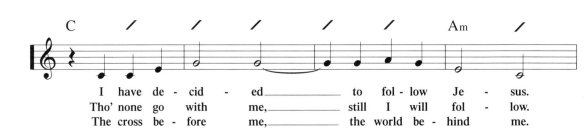

I have de - cid - ed to fol - low Je - sus.
Tho' none go with me, still I will fol - low.
The cross be - fore me, the world be - hind me.

No turn - ing back, no turn - ing back.
No turn - ing back, no turn - ing back.
No turn - ing back, no turn - ing back.

Come Bless the Lord

47

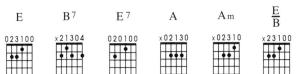

Psalm 134:1, 2

Unknown

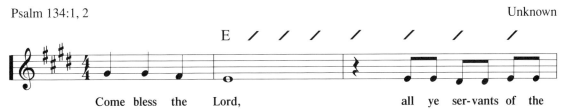

Come bless the Lord, all ye ser-vants of the

Lord Who stand by night

in the house of the Lord! Lift up your

hands in the ho - ly place And bless the

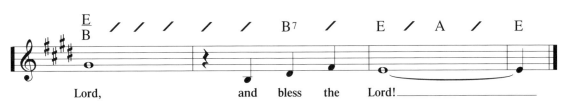

Lord, and bless the Lord!

48 When the Roll Is Called Up Yonder

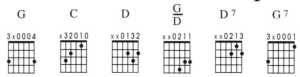

Words and Music by
JAMES M. BLACK

1. When the trum-pet of the Lord shall sound and time shall be no more, And the
2. On that bright and cloud-less morn-ing when the dead in Christ shall rise And the
3. Let us la-bor for the Mas-ter from the dawn till set-ting sun, Let us

morn-ing breaks e-ter-nal, bright, and fair; When the saved of earth shall gath-er o-ver
glo-ry of His res-ur-rec-tion share; When His cho-sen ones shall gath-er to their
talk of all His won-drous love and care; Then when all of life is o-ver and our

on the oth-er shore And the roll is called up yon-der, I'll be there! When the
home be-yond the skies And the roll is called up yon-der, I'll be there!
work on earth is done And the roll is called up yon-der, I'll be there!

Refrain

roll_____ is called up yon-der, When the roll_____ is called up yon-der, When the

roll_____ is called up yon-der, When the roll is called up yon-der I'll be there!

Spring Up, O Well

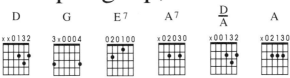

Unknown   Unknown

I've got a riv-er of life flow-ing out of me. It makes the lame to walk and the blind to see; O-pens pris-on doors, sets the cap-tives free. I've got a riv-er of life flow-ing out of me. Spring up, O well, with-in my soul. Spring up, O well, and make me whole. Spring up, O well, and give to me that life a-bun-dant-ly.

The Old Rugged Cross

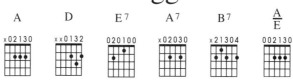

Words and Music by
GEORGE BENNARD

1. On a hill far a - way stood an old rug - ged cross,
2. Oh, that old rug - ged cross, so de - spised by the world,
3. In the old rug - ged cross, stained with blood so di - vine,
4. To the old rug - ged cross I will ev - er be true,

The___ em - blem of suf - f'ring and shame;___
Has a won - drous at - trac - tion for me;___
A___ won - drous beau - ty I see;___
Its___ shame and re - proach glad - ly bear;___

And I love that old cross where the dear - est and best
For the dear Lamb of God left His glo - ry a - bove
For 'twas on that old cross Je - sus suf - fered and died
Then He'll call me some - day to my home far a - way,

For a world of lost sin - ners was slain.___
To___ bear it to dark Cal - va - ry.___
To___ par - don and sanc - ti - fy me.___
Where His glo - ry for - ev - er I'll share.___

Refrain

So I'll cher - ish the old rug - ged cross,___ Till my

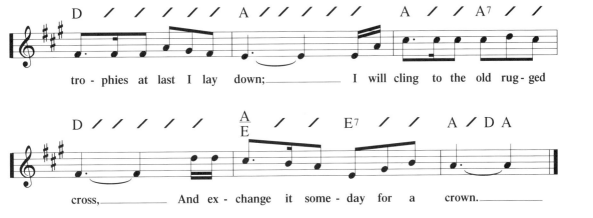

tro - phies at last I lay down;_____ I will cling to the old rug - ged cross,_____ And ex - change it some - day for a crown._____

Lord, We Praise You

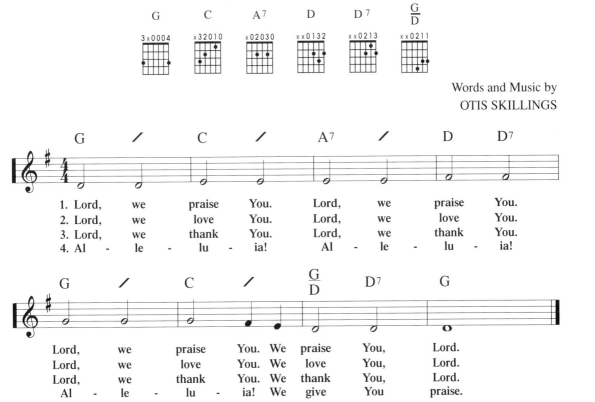

Words and Music by
OTIS SKILLINGS

1. Lord, we praise You. Lord, we praise You.
2. Lord, we love You. Lord, we love You.
3. Lord, we thank You. Lord, we thank You.
4. Al - le - lu - ia! Al - le - lu - ia!

Lord, we praise You. We praise You, Lord.
Lord, we love You. We love You, Lord.
Lord, we thank You. We thank You, Lord.
Al - le - lu - ia! We give You praise.

52 He Giveth More Grace

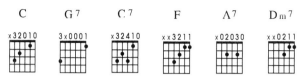

ANNIE JOHNSON FLINT   HUBERT MITCHELL

1. He giv - eth more grace   when the bur - dens grow great - er;   He
2. When we have ex - haust - ed our store of en - dur - ance,   When

send - eth more strength when the la - bors in - crease. To add - ed af - flic - tion He
our strength has failed   ere the day is half done,   When we reach the end of our

add - eth His mer - cy;   To mul - ti - plied tri - als, His   mul - ti - plied peace.
hoard - ed re - sourc - es,   Our Fa - ther's full giv - ing is   on - ly be - gun.

Refrain

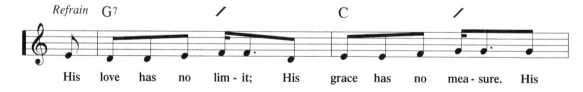

His   love   has   no   lim - it;   His   grace   has   no   mea - sure.   His

pow'r has no bound - a - ry known un - to men.   For   out   of His in - fi - nite

rich - es   in Je - sus, He   giv - eth, and   giv - eth, and   giv - eth a - gain!

Sing Alleluia

53

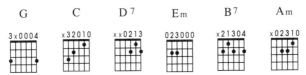

Words and Music by
GARY JOHNSON

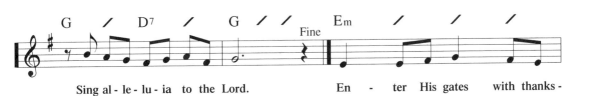

54 Thou Art Worthy

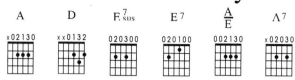

P. M. M., based on Rev. 4:9-11; 5:9-12

PAULINE M. MILLS

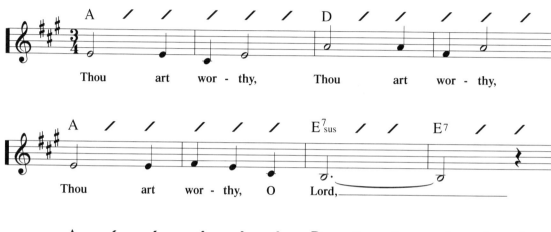

Thou art wor - thy, Thou art wor - thy,

Thou art wor - thy, O Lord, _____

To re - ceive glo - ry, glo - ry and hon - or,

Glo - ry and hon - or and pow'r. _____ For

Thou hast cre - at - ed, hast all things cre - at - ed;

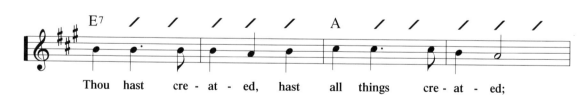

Thou hast cre - at - ed all things. _____

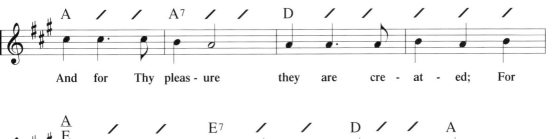

And for Thy pleas-ure they are cre-at-ed; For

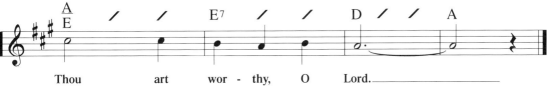

Thou art wor-thy, O Lord.

Praise the Name of Jesus

55

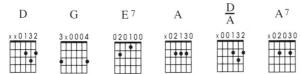

Words and Music by
ROY HICKS, Jr.

Praise the name of Je - sus. Praise the name of Je - sus.

He's my Rock, He's my For - tress, He's my De - liv - er - er; in

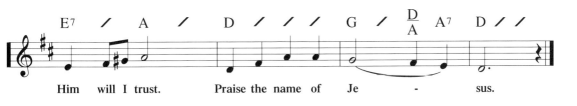

Him will I trust. Praise the name of Je - sus.

56 My Wonderful Lord

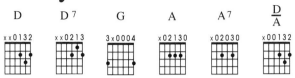

Words and Music by
HALDOR LILLENAS

1. I have found a deep peace that I nev-er had known And a joy this world could not af-ford_____ Since I yield-ed con-trol of my bod-y and soul To my won-der-ful, won-der-ful Lord._____

2. I de-sire that my life shall be or-dered by Thee, That my will be in per-fect ac-cord_____ With Thine own sov-'reign will, Thy de-sires to ful-fill, My won-der-ful, won-der-ful Lord._____

3. All the tal-ents I have I have laid at Thy feet; Thy ap-prov-al shall be my re-ward._____ Be my store great or small, I sur-ren-der it all To my won-der-ful, won-der-ful Lord._____

4. Thou art fair-er to me than the fair-est of earth, Thou om-ni-po-tent, life-giv-ing Word._____ O Thou An-cient of Days, Thou art wor-thy all praise, My won-der-ful, won-der-ful Lord._____

Refrain

My won-der-ful Lord, my won-der-ful Lord, By an-gels and ser-aphs in heav-en a-dored, I bow at Thy shrine, my Sav-ior di-vine, My won-der-ful, won-der-ful Lord._____

Great and Mighty

57

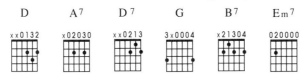

Words and Music by
MARLENE BIGLEY

Great and might - y is the Lord our God,_____ Great and might - y is

He. Great and might - y is the Lord our God,_____

Great and might - y is He. Lift up your ban - ner; let the

an - thems ring_____ Prais - es to our King. Great and might - y is the

Lord our God,_____ Great and might - y is He.

58 I Will Sing of the Mercies of the Lord

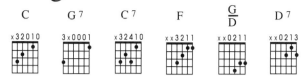

Psalm 89:1

J. H. FILLMORE

I will sing of the mer-cies of the Lord for-ev-er. I will

sing, I will sing. I will sing of the mer-cies of the

Lord for-ev-er. I will sing of the mer-cies of the Lord.

(1st time only) Fine

With my mouth_____ will I make known Thy

faith-ful-ness, Thy faith-ful-ness. With my mouth_____ will I make

D.C. al Fine

known Thy faith-ful-ness to all gen-er-a-tions.

Where He Leads Me

59

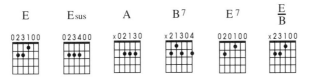

E. W. BLANDY

JOHN S. NORRIS

60 In His Time

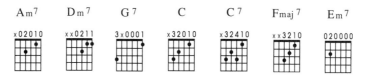

Words and Music by
DIANE BALL

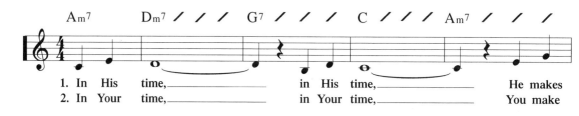

1. In His time,_____ in His time,_____ He makes
2. In Your time,_____ in Your time,_____ You make

all things beau - ti - ful in His time._____ Lord, please
all things beau - ti - ful in Your time._____ Lord, my

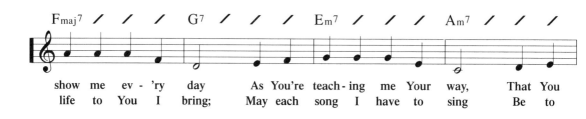

show me ev - 'ry day As You're teach - ing me Your way, That You
life to You I bring; May each song I have to sing Be to

do just as You say in Your time._____
You a love - ly thing in Your time._____

Lord, I Lift Your Name on High

61

Words and Music by
RICK FOUNDS

Lord, I lift Your name on high. Lord, I love to sing Your

prais - es. I'm so glad You're in my life.

I'm so glad You came to save us. You came from heav - en to earth

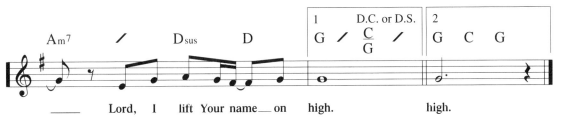

to show the way, From the earth to the cross, my debt to pay.

62 We Have Come into His House

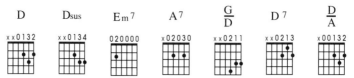

Words and Music by
BRUCE BALLINGER

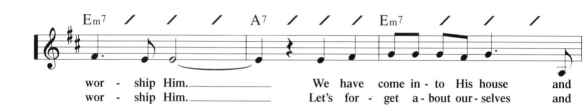

1. We have come in - to His house and gath - ered in His name to
2. Let's for - get a - bout our - selves and mag - ni - fy the Lord and

wor - ship Him. We have come in - to His house and
wor - ship Him. Let's for - get a - bout our - selves and

gath - ered in His name to wor - ship Him. We have
mag - ni - fy the Lord and wor - ship Him. Let's for -

come in - to His house and gath - ered in His name to wor - ship Christ the
get a - bout our - selves and mag - ni - fy the Lord and wor - ship Christ the

Lord. Wor - ship Him– Christ the Lord.
Lord. Wor - ship Him– Christ the Lord.

The Trees of the Field

63

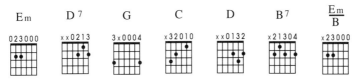

STEFFI GEISER RUBIN, based on Isa. 55:12   STUART DAUERMANN

You shall go out with joy___ and be led forth with peace;___ The

moun-tains and the hills will break forth be-fore you. There'll be shouts of joy_

___ and all the trees of the field Will clap, will clap their hands.

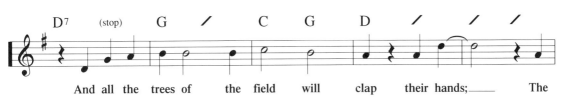

And all the trees of the field will clap their hands;___ The

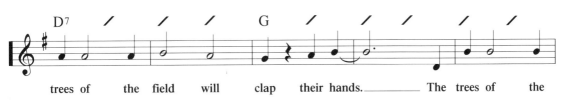

trees of the field will clap their hands.___ The trees of the

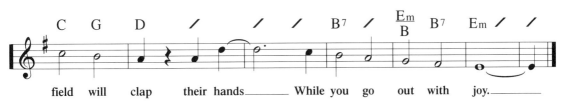

field will clap their hands___ While you go out with joy.___

64 His Grace Is Sufficient for Me

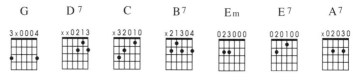

Words and Music by
MOSIE LISTER

1. Man-y times I'm tried and test-ed as I trav-el day by
2. When the tempt-er brings con-fu-sion and I don't know what to

day; Oft I meet with pain and sor-row, and there's trou-ble in the
do, On my knees I turn to Je-sus, for I know He'll see me

way. But I have the sweet as-sur-ance that my soul the Lord will
through. Then de-spair is changed to vic-t'ry; ev-'ry doubt just melts a-

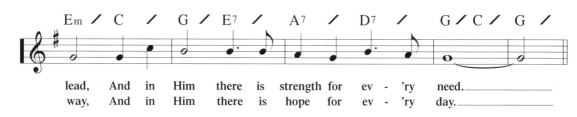

lead, And in Him there is strength for ev-'ry need.____
way, And in Him there is hope for ev-'ry day.____

Refrain

Oh, His grace is suf-fi-cient for____ me,____ And His

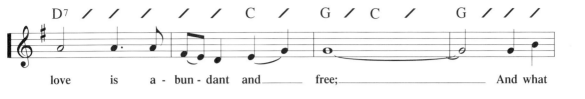

love is a-bun-dant and free; And what

joy fills my soul just to know, just to know That His

grace is suf-fi-cient for me.

Bless the Lord, O My Soul 65

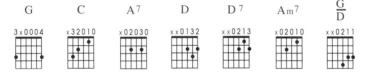

Psalm 103:1   Traditional

Bless the Lord, O my soul; Bless the Lord, O my soul; And

all that is with-in me bless His ho-ly name.

66

To God Be the Glory

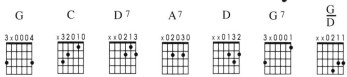

FANNY CROSBY

WILLIAM DOANE

1. To God be the glo - ry– great things He hath done. So loved He the
2. O per - fect re - demp - tion, the pur - chase of blood, To ev - 'ry be -
3. Great things He hath taught us, great things He hath done, And great our re -

world that He gave us His Son, Who yield - ed His life, an a - tone - ment for
liev - er, the prom - ise of God. The vil - est of - fend - er who tru - ly be -
joic - ing thro' Je - sus the Son; But pur - er, and high - er, and great - er will

Refrain

sin, And o - pened the life - gate that all may go in. Praise the
lieves, That mo - ment from Je - sus a par - don re - ceives.
be Our won - der, our trans - port, when Je - sus we see.

Lord, praise the Lord, Let the earth hear His voice! Praise the

Lord, praise the Lord, Let the peo - ple re - joice! O come to the Fa - ther thro'

Je - sus the Son, And give Him the glo - ry– great things He hath done.

We Worship and Adore You

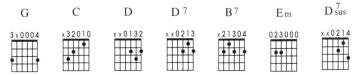

Unknown   Unknown

We wor - ship and a - dore You,

Bow - ing down be - fore You, Songs of prais - es

sing - ing, Hal - le - lu - jahs ring - ing.

Hal - le - lu - jah, hal - le - lu - jah,

Hal - le - lu - jah, a - men.

68 Amazing Grace

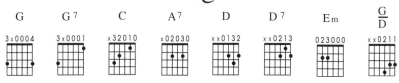

stanzas 1-3, JOHN NEWTON
stanza 4, anonymous

"Virginia Harmony," 1831
Arr. by EDWIN O. EXCELL, 1900

1. A - maz - ing grace! how sweet the sound— That
2. 'Twas grace that taught my heart to fear, And
3. Through man - y dan - gers, toils, and snares I
4. When we've been there ten thou - sand years, Bright

saved a wretch like me! I
grace my fears re - lieved; How
have al - read - y come; 'Tis
shin - ing as the sun, We've

once was lost but now am found, Was
pre - cious did that grace ap - pear The
grace hath bro't me safe thus far, And
no less days to sing God's praise Than

blind but now I see.
hour I first be - lieved.
grace will lead me home.
when we'd first be - gun.

Trust and Obey

69

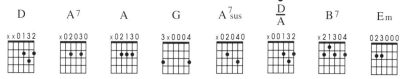

JOHN H. SAMMIS

DANIEL B. TOWNER

1. When we walk with the Lord in the light of His Word, What a
2. Not a bur-den we bear, not a sor-row we share, But our
3. But we nev-er can prove the de-lights of His love Un-til
4. Then in fel-low-ship sweet we will sit at His feet, Or we'll

glo-ry He sheds on our way!_____ While we do His good
toil He doth rich-ly re-pay;_____ Not a grief nor a
all on the al-tar we lay;_____ For the fav-or He
walk by His side in the way;_____ What He says we will

will He a-bides with us still, And with all who will trust and o-bey.
loss, not a frown nor a cross, But is blest if we trust and o-bey.
shows and the joy He be-stows Are for them who will trust and o-bey.
do, where He sends we will go— Nev-er fear, on-ly trust and o-bey.

Refrain

Trust and o-bey, for there's no oth-er way To be

hap-py in Je-sus, but to trust and o-bey.

70 The Bond of Love

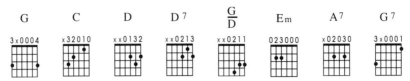

Words and Music by
OTIS SKILLINGS

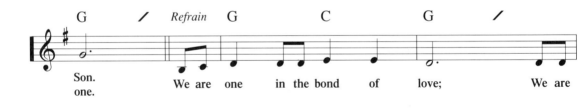

1. Love through Christ has brought us to-geth - er, Melt - ing our hearts as
2. Now, dear Lord, we join in___ wor - ship; Thank You for all You've

one.   By God's Spir - it   we are u - nit - ed; One thro' His bless - ed
done.   Thank You for this   love You gave___ us; Thank You for mak-ing us

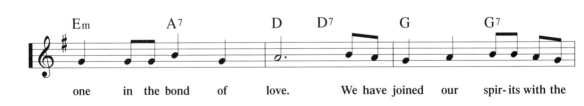

Son.   *Refrain* We are one   in the bond   of   love;   We are
one.

one   in the bond   of   love.   We have joined   our   spir-its with the

Spir - it of God;   We are one   in the bond   of   love.

Hosanna

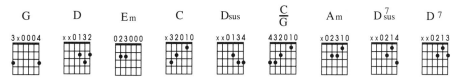

Words and Music by
CARL TUTTLE

1. Ho - san - na, ho - san - na, ho-san-na in the high -
2. ˠ Glo - ry, ˠ glo - ry, ˠ glo-ry to the King of

est; Ho - san - na, ho - san - na, ho-san-na in the high -
Kings; ˠ Glo - ry, ˠ glo - ry, ˠ glo-ry to the King of

est. Lord, we lift up Your name,
Kings.

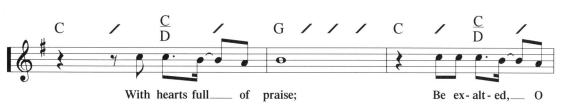

With hearts full of praise; Be ex-alt-ed, O

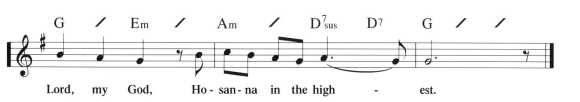

Lord, my God, Ho-san-na in the high - est.

72 'Til the Storm Passes By

Words and Music by
MOSIE LISTER

1. In the dark of the mid-night have I oft hid my face, While the
2. Man-y times Sa-tan whis-pered, "There is no need to try, For there's
3. When the long night has end-ed, and the storms come no more, Let me

storm howls a-bove me, and there's no hid-ing place. 'Mid the crash of the
no end of sor-row; there's no hope by and by." But I know Thou art
stand in Thy pres-ence on that bright peace-ful shore. In that land where the

thun-der, pre-cious Lord, hear my cry, "Keep me safe 'til the
with me, and to-mor-row I'll rise Where the storm nev-er
tem-pest nev-er comes, Lord may I Dwell with Thee when the

Refrain

storm pass-es by." 'Til the storm pass-es o-ver, 'til the
dark-ens the skies.
storm pass-es by.

thun-der sounds no more, 'Til the clouds roll for-ev-er from the

sky, Hold me fast, let me stand in the hol-low of Thy

Lord, Listen to Your Children Praying 73

Words and Music by
KEN MEDEMA

Lord, lis-ten to Your chil-dren pray-ing.

Lord, send Your Spir-it in this place.

Lord, lis-ten to Your chil-dren pray-ing.

___ Send us love, send us pow'r, send us

grace. grace.

74

In the Garden

Words and Music by
C. AUSTIN MILES

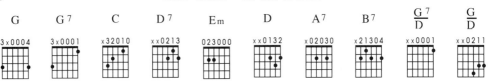

1. I come to the gar-den a-lone,_____ While the dew is still on the
2. He speaks, and the sound of His voice_____ Is so sweet the birds hush their
3. I'd stay in the gar-den with Him_____ Tho' the night a-round me is

ros - es; And the voice I hear fall-ing on my ear The Son of God dis-
sing - ing; And the mel - o - dy that He gave to me With-in my heart is
fall - ing; But He bids me go– thro' the voice of woe, His voice to me is

Refrain

clos - es. And He walks with me, and He talks with me, And He
ring - ing.
call - ing.

tells me I am His own;_____ And the joy we share as we

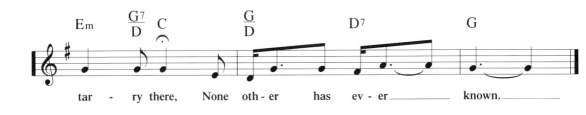

tar - ry there, None oth - er has ev - er_____ known.

Change My Heart, O God

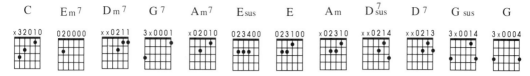

Words and Music by
EDDIE ESPINOSA

Change my heart, O God,_____ Make it ev - er true.

_____ Change my heart, O God,_____

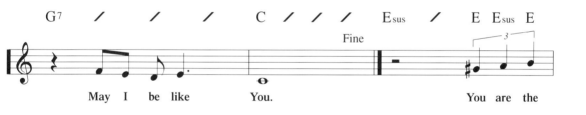

May I be like You. You are the

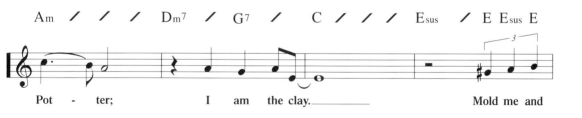

Pot - ter; I am the clay._____ Mold me and

make_____ me; this is what I_____ pray.

Chord Diagrams

Illustrating all of the chords used in this book

x = do not play this string   **0** = open string

Note that many chords do not use all six strings of the guitar. For example, for the "A" chord, the "**x**" indicates that the sixth string is not played. So to play the "A" chord, begin strumming from the fifth string (the "A" string). Chords such as $\frac{A}{E}$ indicates that a note other than the root of the chord is in the bass. In this case the sixth string (the "E" string) would be played.

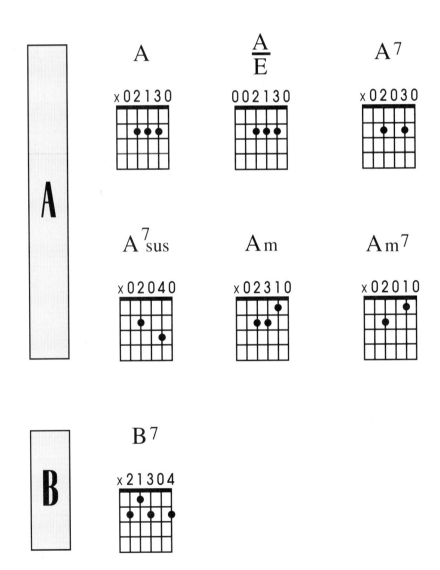

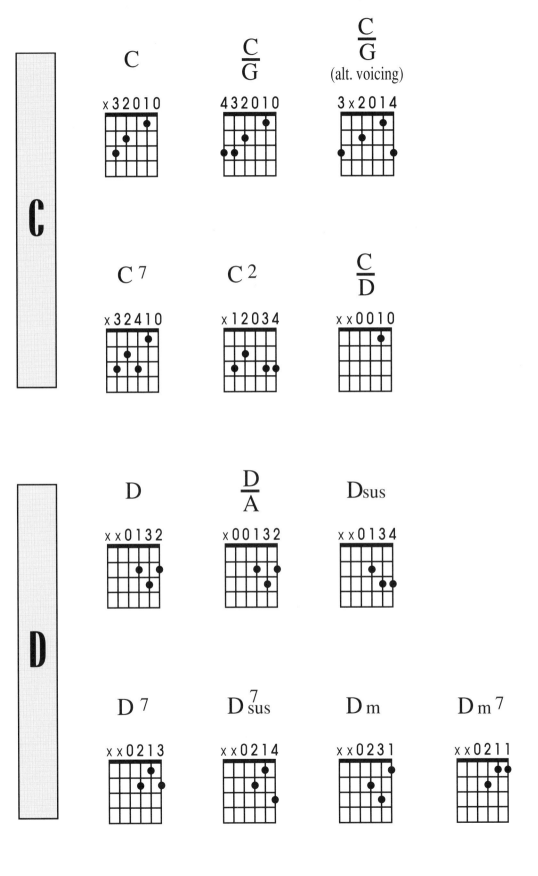

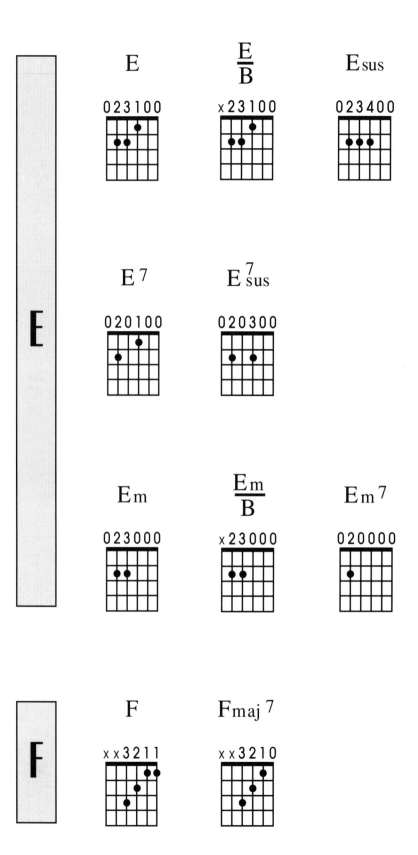

G

G (easy)

x x 0 0 0 3

Use this fingering when first learning the "G" chord.

G

3 2 0 0 0 4

Standard fingering for the "G" chord.

G

3 x 0 0 0 4

Editor's preferred fingering (gives a clear, ringing tone). The third finger should touch the fifth string to deaden or mute the sound.

G (alt. voicing)

2 1 0 0 3 4

This fingering used on "Take My Life".

G sus

3 x 0 0 1 4

The third finger should touch the fifth string to deaden or mute the sound.

$\frac{G}{D}$

x x 0 2 1 1

G 7

3 2 0 0 0 1

Standard fingering for the "G7" chord.

G 7

3 x 0 0 0 1

Editor's preferred fingering. The third finger should touch the fifth string to deaden or mute the sound.

$\frac{G7}{D}$

x x 0 0 0 1

A SUGGESTED ORDER OF STUDY

By following this order, you will learn one chord (or in a few cases, two) at a time, as applied to songs from this book. And, in each new song, you will use chords you have learned previously, thus building knowledge with each new song. Refer to the index of chord diagrams to learn how to make the chords.

NOTE: after completing this study, you will have learned 36 chords and 46 songs.

D A^7	Oh, How I Love Jesus	3
	Bind Us Together	2
G (easy)	Through It All	11
	Behold What Manner of Love	8
$\frac{D}{A}$	It Is a Good Thing to Give Thanks	16
	The Joy of the Lord	28
D^7	Shall We Gather at the River?	29
	God Is So Good	35
Em	This Is My Commandment	27
	I've Been Redeemed	20
$\frac{G}{D}$	Have Thine Own Way, Lord	32
Em^7	I Will Bless Thee, O Lord	25
A$^7_{sus}$	At the Cross	31
E^7	I Will Bless the Lord at All Times	41
A	Down in My Heart	18
	There Is Power in the Blood	26
$\frac{A}{E}$	There Is a Fountain	42
E$^7_{sus}$	Thou Art Worthy	54
B^7	King of Kings	5

E	Rejoice in the Lord Always	1
	Father, I Adore You	15
$\frac{E}{B}$	Nothing But the Blood	13
	Only Trust Him	19
A m	Come Bless the Lord	47
C	Alleluia	14
	Leaning on the Everlasting Arms	45
G	Are You Washed in the Blood?	34
	The Unclouded Day	12
G^7	Hallowed Be Thy Name	4
A m^7	Hallelu, Hallelujah!	36
F	This Little Light of Mine	7
	Savior, Like a Shepherd Lead Us	10
C^7	I Will Sing of the Mercies of the Lord	58
$\frac{C}{G}$	Jesus Loves Me	40
	I Have Decided to Follow Jesus	46
D m^7	He Giveth More Grace	52
F maj^7	In His Time	60
D m	Emmanuel	33
	Kum Ba Yah	37
G C^2 (alt. voicing)	Take My Life	24
D sus	We Have Come into His House	62
$\frac{C}{G}$	Lord, I Lift Your Name on High	61
D^7 sus	We Worship and Adore You	67
$\frac{C}{D}$	Hosanna	71
$\frac{G^7}{D}$	In the Garden	74
E sus G sus	Change My Heart, O God	75

SONG TYPE INDEX

CHORUS / SCRIPTURE SONG

Alleluia 14
Behold What Manner of Love 8
Bind Us Together 2
Bless the Lord, O My Soul 65
Change My Heart, O God 75
Come Bless the Lord 47
Emmanuel 33
Father, I Adore You 15
God Is So Good 35
Great and Mighty 57
Hallowed Be Thy Name 4
Hosanna 71
I Have Decided to Follow Jesus 46
I Will Bless the Lord at All Times 41
I Will Bless Thee, O Lord 25
I Will Sing of the Mercies of the Lord 58
In His Time 60
It Is a Good Thing to Give Thanks 16
King of Kings 5
Kum Ba Yah 37
Lord, I Lift Your Name on High 61
Lord, Listen to Your Children Praying 73
Lord, We Praise You 51
Peace like a River 38
Praise the Name of Jesus 55
Rejoice in the Lord Always 1
Servant of All 6
Spring Up, O Well 49
Take My Life 24
The Battle Belongs to the Lord 22
The Bond of Love 70
The Joy of the Lord 28
The Trees of the Field 63
They'll Know We Are Christians 30
This Is My Commandment 27
Thou Art Worthy 54
Through It All 11
Thy Loving Kindness 44
Unto Thee, O Lord 21
We Have Come into His House 62
We Worship and Adore You 67

CHILDREN'S SONG

Down in My Heart 18

God Is So Good 35
Hallelu, Hallelujah! 36
I Have Decided to Follow Jesus 46
I Will Sing of the Mercies of the Lord 58
I've Been Redeemed 20
Jesus Loves Me 40
Kum Ba Yah 37
Oh, How I Love Jesus 3
Peace like a River 38
Rejoice in the Lord Always 1
Sing Alleluia 53
Spring Up, O Well 49
The Joy of the Lord 28
This Is My Commandment 27
This Little Light of Mine 7

HYMN / GOSPEL SONG

Amazing Grace 68
Are You Washed in the Blood? 34
At the Cross 31
Have Thine Own Way, Lord 32
He Giveth More Grace 52
Higher Ground 17
His Grace Is Sufficient for Me 64
In the Garden 74
Leaning on the Everlasting Arms 45
My Wonderful Lord 56
Nothing But the Blood 13
Oh, How I Love Jesus 3
Only Trust Him 1 9
Redeemed 9
Revive Us Again 23
Savior, Like a Shepherd Lead Us 10
Shall We Gather at the River? 29
Sweet By and By 39
The Old Rugged Cross 50
The Unclouded Day 12
There Is a Fountain 42
There Is Power in the Blood 26
'Til the Storm Passes By 72
To God Be the Glory 66
Trust and Obey 69
What a Friend We Have in Jesus 43
When the Roll Is Called Up Yonder 48
Where He Leads Me 59

KEY INDEX

Key of A

Down in My Heart 18
The Old Rugged Cross 50
There Is a Fountain 42
There Is Power in the Blood 26
Thou Art Worthy 54

Key of C

Change My Heart, O God 75
Emmanuel 33
Hallowed Be Thy Name 4
He Giveth More Grace 52
I Have Decided to Follow Jesus 46
I Will Sing of the Mercies of the Lord 58
In His Time 60
Jesus Loves Me 40
Kum Ba Yah 37
Savior, Like a Shepherd Lead Us 10
This Little Light of Mine 7
'Til the Storm Passes By 72

Key of D

At the Cross 31
Behold What Manner of Love 8
Bind Us Together 2
God Is So Good 35
Great and Mighty 57
Have Thine Own Way, Lord 32
I Will Bless the Lord at All Times 41
I Will Bless Thee, O Lord 25
It Is a Good Thing to Give Thanks 16
I've Been Redeemed 20
Lord, Listen to Your Children Praying 73
My Wonderful Lord 56
Oh, How I Love Jesus 3
Praise the Name of Jesus 55
Servant of All 6
Shall We Gather at the River? 29
Spring Up, O Well 49
The Joy of the Lord 28
This Is My Commandment 27
Through It All 11
Thy Loving Kindness 44

Trust and Obey 69
We Have Come into His House 62

Key of E

Come Bless the Lord 47
Father, I Adore You 15
Nothing But the Blood 13
Only Trust Him 19
Peace like a River 38
Rejoice in the Lord Always 1
Revive Us Again 23
Sweet By and By 39
Unto Thee, O Lord 21
What a Friend We Have in Jesus 43
Where He Leads Me 59

Key of G

Alleluia 14
Amazing Grace 68
Are You Washed in the Blood? 34
Bless the Lord, O My Soul 65
Hallelu, Hallelujah! 36
Higher Ground 17
His Grace Is Sufficient for Me 64
Hosanna 71
In the Garden 74
Leaning on the Everlasting Arms 45
Lord, I Lift Your Name on High 61
Lord, We Praise You 51
Redeemed 9
Sing Alleluia 53
Take My Life 24
The Bond of Love 70
The Unclouded Day 12
To God Be the Glory 66
We Worship and Adore You 67
When the Roll Is Called Up Yonder 48

Key of Em

King of Kings 5
The Battle Belongs to the Lord 22
The Trees of the Field 63
They'll Know We Are Christians 30

ALPHA INDEX

	TITLE	NUMBER	KEY	#CHORDS
	Alleluia	14	G	3
	Amazing Grace	68	G	8
	Are You Washed in the Blood?	34	G	5
	At the Cross	31	D	5
	Behold What Manner of Love	8	D	3
	Bind Us Together	2	D	2
	Bless the Lord, O My Soul	65	G	7
	Change My Heart, O God	75	C	12
	Come Bless the Lord	47	E	6
COPY	Down in My Heart	18	A	4
	Emmanuel	33	C	5
	Father, I Adore You	15	E	3
	God Is So Good	35	D	5
	Great and Mighty	57	D	6
COPY	Hallelu, Hallelujah!	36	G	5
	Hallowed Be Thy Name	4	C	2
	Have Thine Own Way, Lord	32	D	5
	He Giveth More Grace	52	C	6
	Higher Ground	17	G	4
	His Grace Is Sufficient for Me	64	G	7
COPY	Hosanna	71	G	9
COPY	I Have Decided to Follow Jesus	46	C	6
	I Will Bless the Lord at All Times	41	D	5
	I Will Bless Thee, O Lord	25	D	4
	I Will Sing of the Mercies of the Lord	58	C	6
	In His Time	60	C	7
	In the Garden	74	G	10
	It Is a Good Thing to Give Thanks	16	D	4
	I've Been Redeemed	20	D	4
	Jesus Loves Me	40	C	5
	King of Kings	5	Em	2
Copy	Kum Ba Yah	37	C	5
	Leaning on the Everlasting Arms	45	G	5
	Lord, I Lift Your Name on High	61	G	7

Lord, Listen to Your Children Praying 73	D	9
Lord, We Praise You 51	G	6
My Wonderful Lord 56	D	6
Nothing But the Blood 13	E	3
Oh, How I Love Jesus 3	D	2
Only Trust Him 19	E	4
Peace like a River 38	E	5
Praise the Name of Jesus 55	D	6
Redeemed 9	G	3
Rejoice in the Lord Always 1	E	2
Revive Us Again 23	E	4
Savior, Like a Shepherd Lead Us 10	C	3
Servant of All 6	D	3
Shall We Gather at the River? 29	D	4
Sing Alleluia 53	G	6
Spring Up, O Well 49	D	6
Sweet By and By 39	E	5
Take My Life 24	G	4
The Battle Belongs to the Lord 22	Em	4
The Bond of Love 70	G	8
The Joy of the Lord 28	D	4
The Old Rugged Cross 50	A	6
The Trees of the Field 63	Em	7
The Unclouded Day 12	G	3
There Is a Fountain 42	A	5
There Is Power in the Blood 26	A	4
They'll Know We Are Christians 30	Em	4
This Is My Commandment 27	D	4
This Little Light of Mine 7	C	3
Thou Art Worthy 54	A	6
Through It All 11	D	3
Thy Loving Kindness 44	D	5
'Til the Storm Passes By 72	C	9
To God Be the Glory 66	G	7
Trust and Obey 69	D	8
Unto Thee, O Lord 21	E	4
We Have Come into His House 62	D	7
We Worship and Adore You 67	G	7
What a Friend We Have in Jesus 43	E	5
When the Roll Is Called Up Yonder 48	G	6
Where He Leads Me 59	E	6